THINGS YOU SHOULD KNOW ABOUT

BEARS

By Steve Parker
Illustrated by Andrea Morandi

BARDFIELD
PRESS

First published by Bardfield Press in 2006
Copyright © Miles Kelly Publishing Ltd 2006

Bardfield Press is an imprint of
Miles Kelly Publishing Ltd
Bardfield Centre
Great Bardfield
Essex, CM7 4SL

2 4 6 8 10 9 7 5 3 1

Editorial Director: Belinda Gallagher
Art Director: Jo Brewer
Designer: HERRINGBONE DESIGN
Production: Elizabeth Brunwin
Reprographics: Mike Coupe, Stephan Davis
Indexer: Jane Parker

ISBN 1-84236-748-X

Printed in China

www.mileskelly.net
info@mileskelly.net

British Library Cataloguing-in-Publication Data
A catalogue record for this book is available
from the British Library

Contents

Bears go fishing

Bear facts

- The biggest male brown bears stand nearly 3 metres tall and weigh over 600 kilograms.
- Females are about half the size of males.
- Brown bears live in all northern lands, but mainly in remote places.

The **BROWN BEAR** rivals the polar bear as the world's biggest meat-eating land animal. It does not eat just meat. It loves fish, grubs, birds' eggs, honey from wild bees' nests, fruits, berries — in fact, just about anything. The brown bear is always hungry!

The brown bear waits for leaping salmon that swim upstream to breed. It catches them in its powerful jaws or hooks them out with its massive paws.

The brown bear enjoys feasts of fish and fruits during autumn. It puts on huge amounts of weight as layers of body fat. This is stored food to last through the long cold season.

By spring, after its long winter sleep, the bear has lost half of its body weight.

Not all brown bears are brown. Some are light grey or cream, while others are chocolate-coloured or even almost black.

Grizzled grizzly

Brown bears are called grizzlies. Their fur has white tips, making them look old, grey and 'grizzled'.

Bears go nuts!

Bear facts

- The Asian black bear is about 1.7 metres long.
- It weighs 100 to 200 kilograms.
- It lives across Asia, except for the far north and the Indian region.

Most bears eat a huge range of foods, including meat and plants. The **ASIAN BLACK BEAR** loves nuts — beechnuts, hazelnuts, walnuts, chestnuts and pinenuts. However, sometimes this bear will eat crops such as maize (sweetcorn). Then it is not the farmer's best friend.

Moon bear

The Asian black bear has a pale chest patch shaped like a V or U. This is why it is also known as the 'moon bear'.

The Asian black bear usually visits the farmer's maize fields on moonlit nights. Otherwise it prefers to live and feed in the forest.

The maize cobs are torn off by the bear's long teeth, called canines.

The Asian black bear also eats bamboo – and so does its cousin the giant panda. But the two usually avoid each other and rarely meet.

This bear can also be found in the Himalayan Mountains, where it is known as the Himalayan bear.

Some bears wear glasses!

Bear facts
• The spectacled bear is the only bear living in South America.
• It lives mainly in the forests of the Andes Mountains.
• It is up to 2 metres long and weighs 140 kilograms.

Of all the bears, the **SPECTACLED BEAR** spends most of its time in trees. It climbs by wrapping its four legs around the trunk in a 'bear hug' and then it shuffles upwards, faster than you could walk! Pale eye patches give this bear its name – spectacled. It is also called the Andean bear.

Big-eyed bear

Each spectacled bear has its own shape of eye patches. Some have small spots, others whole circles.

Like most bears, the spectacled bear lives to the age of 20 or perhaps 25 years.

Bears have long noses and an excellent sense of smell. Their hearing is also very good. But their eyes are small and they probably cannot see quite as well as we can.

Bears often stand up to look, listen and sniff for food or danger.

The spectacled bear pulls down low-growing branches so it can eat the fruits, berries or soft bark.

The spectacled bear is becoming rarer. People disturb its natural home as they take over wild areas for farmland or leisure.

Baby bears are tiny

Bear facts
- The American black bear lives in many places in North America, from frozen Alaska to hot Mexico.
- It is up to 2 metres long and weighs 300 kilograms.

A mother bear is huge, but her new babies, or cubs, are tiny. When the newborn cubs of the **AMERICAN BLACK BEAR** are curled up asleep, each is hardly bigger than your fist. Their eyes are closed, they cannot hear and they have little fur. But they grow fast. Soon the cubs can crawl about and squeak inside their safe den. When they get bigger, it is time to go outside.

The cubs are born in winter. Their den is in a cave or among the roots of a tree. The mother lines it with grass and leaves, so it is warm and comfortable.

Bear legs!
Make a walking bear from pieces of card, fixed with split-pins so the legs move. Can it walk and wave at the same time?

By watching their mother, the cubs learn how to find food and discover what is good to eat.

The cubs stay near their mother for the first year of their lives. She protects them from danger such as wolves and eagles.

Bears love honey

Bear facts

Bear facts
- The sun bear is about 1.2 metres long and weighs 50 kilograms.
- It lives mainly in the forests of Southeast Asia.

The **SUN BEAR** is the smallest kind of bear. It is about the size of a big dog, but much more powerful, with strong muscles, dangerous teeth and long claws. It also has the shortest fur of any bear. This bear loves honey so much, that it is sometimes called the 'honey bear'.

Long tongue

The sun bear's tongue stretches out 25 centimetres to lick food out of cracks. How long is your tongue?

All bears can climb well, but some of the bigger kinds are too heavy. The sun bear is lighter and spends much of its time in the branches.

This bear's fur varies from black to grey or rusty-brown. The rounded patch on its chest is orange or yellow – like the rising sun.

The bear tears open a bees' nest with its claws, scoops out the honeycomb with its paws and quickly licks up the honey.

Most bears have tails – but only just. The tail is very small and is often hidden in the fur of the rear end. It is not much use, except for sitting on!

Some bears snore

The **EURASIAN BROWN BEAR** is a type of brown bear that lives across Europe and Asia. In the far north, where winters are long and cold, it sleeps for weeks on end. In warmer southern parts it sleeps much less.

The winter den is in a favourite rocky cave, or a large hole in a bank or under a log. The bear may sleep on and off for up to six months!

Bear facts
• The Eurasian brown bear is massive, but not quite as big as other brown bears such as the Kodiak bear (see page 20).
• Some live as far south as the hot lands of the Middle East.

Big-foot
Bears leave tracks in snow, sand and mud. They are huge, each with a rounded paw and five long claws.

The sleeping bear curls up to keep warm, and breathes very slowly. Sometimes it snores! It can wake up quickly if there is danger, such as a flood.

During winter, the bear does not sleep all the time. It may wake up on milder days, and wander about in search of a drink and a snack — and go to the toilet. Then it settles down to snooze again.

Bears rarely share

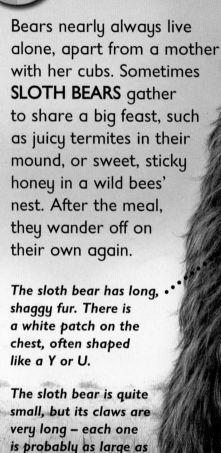

Bear facts

- The sloth bear lives in India and nearby regions.
- It stays mainly in forests and avoids open places.
- It is quite small compared to other bears, and measures 1.6 metres in length.

Bears nearly always live alone, apart from a mother with her cubs. Sometimes **SLOTH BEARS** gather to share a big feast, such as juicy termites in their mound, or sweet, sticky honey in a wild bees' nest. After the meal, they wander off on their own again.

The sloth bear has long, shaggy fur. There is a white patch on the chest, often shaped like a Y or U.

The sloth bear is quite small, but its claws are very long – each one is probably as large as your whole finger. The front claws are longer than the back ones.

Long claws are excellent for digging up ants, termites and grubs, but not so good for climbing. Sloth bears usually run from enemies rather than climb a tree.

This bear's lips are strong, and it sucks up ants or termites one by one. The sucking is so noisy, it can be heard from 100 metres away!

Hang on, junior!

The baby sloth bear rides 'bear-back' on its mother. She has a special patch of fur there, so the cub can hang on more easily.

Sloth bears are named because they move slowly – just like real sloths. But if they are in danger, they may strike out with their long, sharp claws.

Rare bear

Bear facts
- Giant pandas live in small areas of southwest China.
- Their bamboo forest homes are high in the hills.
- An adult giant panda measures 1.8 metres in length and weighs 100 kilograms.

The **GIANT PANDA** is an extremely rare animal. There are only about 1000 left living in the wild, all in China. This bear is famous for eating just one food – bamboo, a type of fast-growing, woody grass. But sometimes the panda snacks on different foods.

A panda may raid a bird's nest for eggs, or catch a lizard or mouse, or even eat the meat from a dead animal such as a forest pig. But most of its food, 99 meals out of 100, is bamboo.

Bears rarely make noises. Pandas can groan like a whale, bark like a dog and bleat like a sheep! This happens when they try to avoid each other, or when a male and female get together to mate.

People once thought giant pandas were related to raccoons. Scientists now know that they are members of the bear family. These endangered creatures need our help to survive.

Six fingers?

The panda seems to have six fingers. But the extra one is really part of its wrist. It helps it to hold food.

Bear facts

• Kodiak bears weigh most in autumn, as they feed on plentiful fruits, berries and fish.

• They can sprint at over 30 kilometres an hour – that is faster than most humans!

The brown bears called **KODIAK BEARS** are the biggest land hunters. They can weigh almost one tonne! They live on Kodiak Island, off the south coast of Alaska, in the far northwest of North America. Most of Kodiak Island is a nature reserve where bears and other creatures live and feed in peace.

Tall and small

A Kodiak bear may stand almost twice as high as a person – and weigh ten times as much.

A bear has small front teeth called incisors for nibbling and nipping, and long canine teeth for stabbing and tearing. Its back teeth, or molars, are wide, for chewing.

Bears such as the Kodiak roam a regular area called their home range. They leave smelly droppings and urine, and scratch marks on trees, to tell other bears of their presence.

If two bears meet, they usually ignore each other and go their separate ways. Unless it is the breeding season!

Some bears like ice

Bear facts

- A male polar bear is about 3 metres long and weighs half a tonne.
- As in most bears, the female is smaller, about two-thirds of the male's size.
- Polar bears live all around the Arctic.

The **POLAR BEAR** is one of the biggest bears — almost equally as massive as the brown bear. It is also the fiercest, because it does much more hunting than the other types of bear, and eats far fewer fruits, berries or plants.

The polar bear is at home in the water, as well as on land. It paddles fast with its massive front paws and can swim for many hours.

Polar bears eat many animals, especially seals, small whales, seabirds and their eggs, caribou (reindeer) and even rats!

The baby polar bear is born in midwinter, in a den dug in the snow. It stays there with its mother for three months.

White fur helps to camouflage the polar bear, so it blends in with the ice and snow of its Arctic home. Its thick fur and a layer of fat under its skin keep the bear very warm.

Wait for dinner

A polar bear may wait hours for a seal to visit its breathing hole. Then the bear grabs the seal as it surfaces.

At first, the cub feeds on its mother's milk. From the age of five months it shares its mother's food. Then it begins to hunt for its own meals. By the age of two and a half years, the young bear has left its mother to live alone.

The polar bear cub learns to swim with its mother. Male bears never take part in caring for their cubs. In fact males sometimes try to kill them!

Index